HOORAY FOR DOCTORS!

by Tessa Kenan

BUMBA BOOKS™

LERNER PUBLICATIONS ◆ MINNEAPOLIS

Note to Educators:

Throughout this book, you'll find critical thinking questions. These can be used to engage young readers in thinking critically about the topic and in using the text and photos to do so.

Lerner Publications Company
A division of Lerner Publishing Group, Inc.
241 First Avenue North
Minneapolis, MN 55401 USA

For reading levels and more information, look up this title at www.lernerbooks.com.

Library of Congress Cataloging-in-Publication Data

Names: Kenan, Tessa, author.
Title: Hooray for doctors! / by Tessa Kenan.
Other titles: Hooray for community helpers!
Description: Minneapolis : Lerner Publications, [2018] | Series: Bumba books. Hooray for community helpers! | Audience: Ages 4–7. | Audience: K to grade 3. | Includes bibliographical references and index.
Identifiers: LCCN 2016054411 (print) | LCCN 2017006557 (ebook) | ISBN 9781512433500 (lb : alk. paper) | ISBN 9781512455502 (pb : alk. paper) | ISBN 9781512450323 (eb pdf)
Subjects: LCSH: Physicians—Juvenile literature.
Classification: LCC R690 .K457 2018 (print) | LCC R690 (ebook) | DDC 610.69/5—dc23

LC record available at https://lccn.loc.gov/2016054411

Manufactured in the United States of America
1 — CG — 7/15/17

Expand learning beyond the printed book. Download free, complementary educational resources for this book from our website, www.lerneresource.com.

Table of
Contents

Doctors Care for Patients

Doctors work in hospitals and clinics.

They keep patients healthy.

They help patients who are sick

or hurt.

Doctors work with nurses.

They treat patients together.

There are many kinds of doctors.

Some doctors help new mothers.

Others fix broken bones.

Many doctors wear white coats.

They may wear face masks.

These protect them from germs.

Why do
you think a
doctor's coat
is white?

Some doctors perform

surgeries.

They wear scrubs.

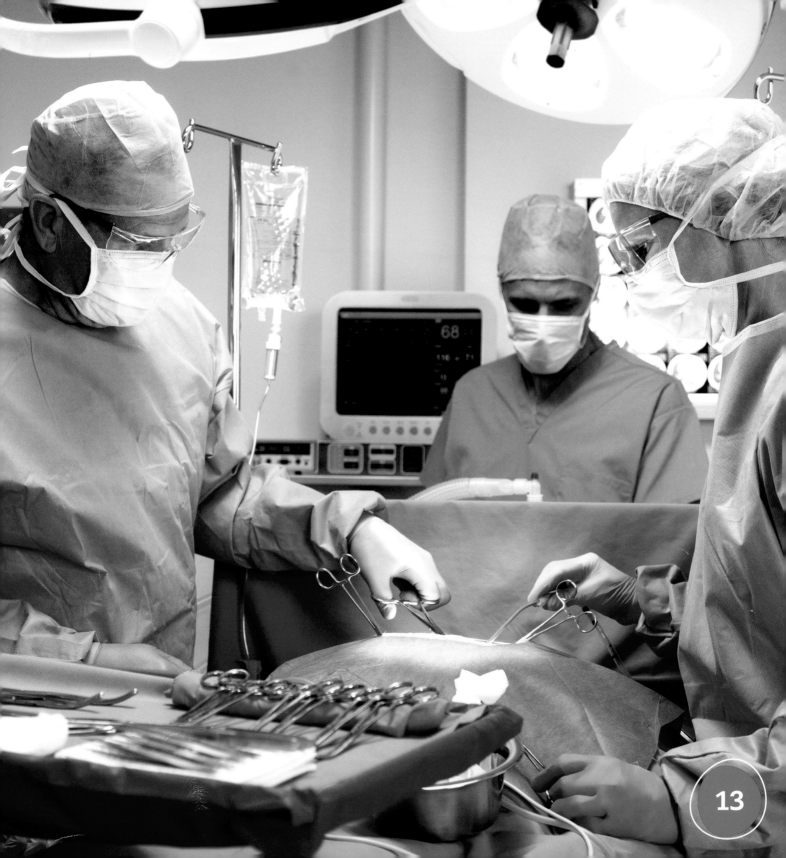

Doctors use tools.

This is a stethoscope.

The doctor uses it to listen to the

patient's heartbeat.

What other tools might a doctor use?

Doctors ask questions.

They decide what a patient needs.

This patient needs a shot.

Doctors go to school for a long time.

Each doctor goes to school for at least eleven years!

Why must doctors go to school?

19

Doctors work long hours.

Some work during the night.

They work hard to care

for people.

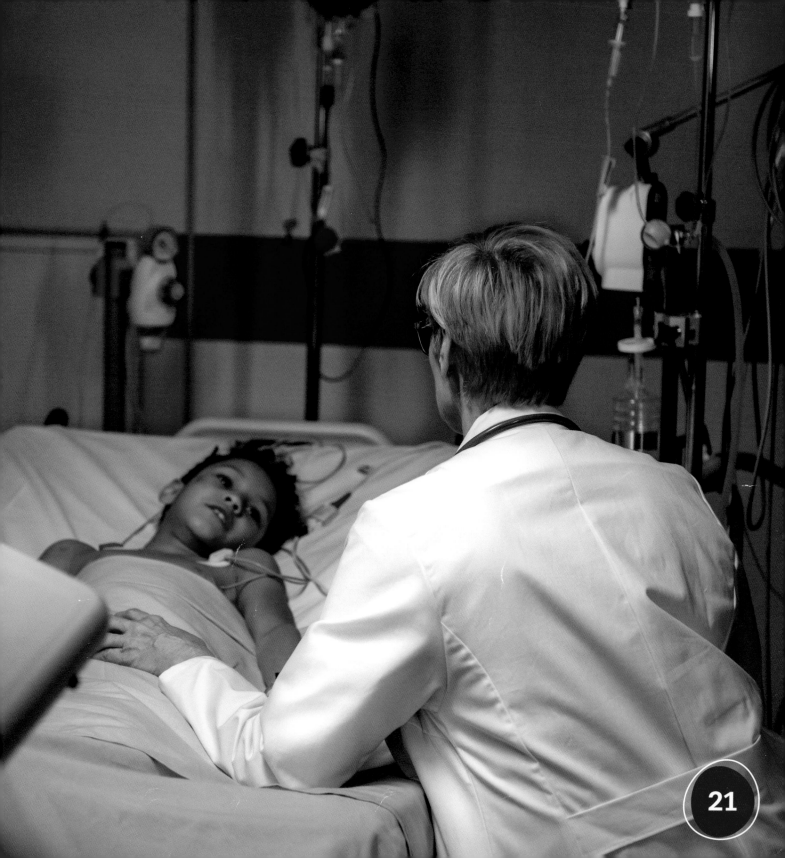

Doctor Tools

face mask

stethoscope

coat

Picture Glossary

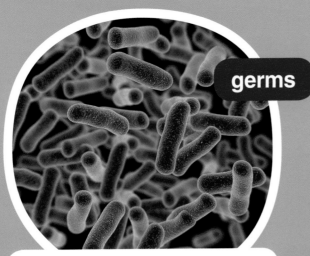

germs

small, living things that make people sick

patients

sick or hurt people treated by nurses and doctors

stethoscope

a tool used to listen to someone's heart or lungs

surgeries

procedures where doctors open up part of someone's body to fix it

23

Read More

Bellamy, Adam. *This Is My Doctor.* New York: Enslow Publishing, 2017.

Heos, Bridget. *Let's Meet a Doctor.* Minneapolis: Millbrook Press, 2013.

Miller, Connie Colwell. *I'll Be a Doctor.* Mankato, MN: Amicus Illustrated, 2017.

Index

Photo Credits